Mentor Guide

The Trainer
Development
Programme

Developed in
collaboration with

THE INSTITUTE OF TRAINING
AND DEVELOPMENT
and
THAMES VALLEY UNIVERSITY
LONDON

and published by

PERGAMON OPEN LEARNING
a division of
Elsevier Science Ltd

MENTOR GUIDE

U.K.	Elsevier Science Ltd, The Boulevard, Langford Lane, Kidlington, Oxford, OX5 1GB, England
U.S.A.	Elsevier Science Inc, 660 White Plains Road, Tarrytown, New York, 10591-5153, USA
JAPAN	Elsevier Science Japan, Tsunashima Building Annex, 3-20-12 Yushima, Bunkyo-ku, Tokyo 113, Japan

First published 1994
Reprinted 1994

A catalogue record for this book is available from the British Library.

ISBN: 0-08-042171-7

The views expressed in this work are those of the authors and do not necessarily reflect those of the Institute of Training and Development, Thames Valley University – London, or the publisher.

All names are purely fictitious and any resemblance to real people, companies and events throughout the text and on the audio cassette is purely coincidental.

AUTHORS:
Jan Chapell and Celia Wathen

PROJECT MANAGEMENT:
Pergamon Open Learning

WRITING TEAM MANAGEMENT AND COORDINATION:
Tad Leduchowicz, Thames Valley University – London

ITD PROJECT MANAGEMENT AND COORDINATION:
Margaret Sands, Institute of Training and Development

REVIEW CONSULTANT FOR ITD:
Roger Bennett of The Management Development Consultancy

EDITORIAL CONSULTANT:
Sally Jefferies of Optima Open Learning

DESIGN AND PRODUCTION MANAGEMENT:
Pergamon Open Learning

TYPOGRAPHIC DESIGN:
op den Brouw Design and Illustration Consultancy, Reading, England

Printed and bound by The Charlesworth Group, Huddersfield, England

Contents

INTRODUCTION

The *Trainer Development Programme* has been designed by the Institute of Training and Development, Thames Valley University and publishers, Pergamon Open Learning.

The *Programme* gives users the opportunity to develop knowledge and skills which are directly relevant to their own jobs in a training and development environment. The overall aims of the *Programme* are:

- to develop the skills required for effective learning and training, by providing knowledge, understanding and guided practice;

- to help learners obtain recognised qualifications in training and development.

This booklet has been developed as a supplement to the *Programme* and gives guidance as to how mentors can help and support people undertaking this programme.

Once you have worked through this booklet, as a mentor you will be better able to:

- describe the *Programme* to the learner;

- use good mentoring practice to guide a learner through the *Programme* and the S/NVQ system;

- identify the role and responsibilities of a mentor;

- provide the support needed by a learner taking part in an open learning programme and explain why this support is essential.

Other useful sources of information

The programme includes two other items that should help you in your role as a mentor:

- *User Guide*, which introduces learners to the *Programme* and helps them to plan their course of study;

- Module TDS 6 *Mentoring*, which examines the process of mentoring and the skills involved from a variety of different perspectives, and includes a number of Workplace Activities to encourage good practice.

You are encouraged to have these items by your side and to consult them as sources of further information and clarification when required.

PART 1

How to be an Effective Mentor

INTRODUCTION

As a mentor there are several things you need to know about providing support to someone who is undertaking the *Trainer Development Programme*. This booklet is designed to provide you with that information – but first you may well be asking "What is a mentor?" and "What sort of support is a mentor supposed to provide?", so we will try to answer these questions first.

1.1 WHAT IS A MENTOR?

The dictionary definition of a mentor is an 'experienced and trusted advisor and guide' (after Mentor, who was the person entrusted by Odysseus to be tutor to his household). The use of mentoring as a developmental tool is therefore not new. In fact, it has been used for many years, such as in apprenticeship training when master craftsmen took responsibility for nurturing youngsters under their control. Such relationships have not just been limited to craftsmen's guilds however. Managers have always 'kept an eye on' high flyers, supervisors have always taken new recruits 'under their wing', and so on. With the increasing importance of work-based S/NVQ qualifications, the use of mentors has become even more widespread and they are now regarded as one of the most important sources of support and advice for anyone undertaking a serious training programme.

The key role of the mentor in the *Trainer Development Programme* is therefore to ensure that the learner to whom they are acting as mentor gets the most out of the programme, not only for the benefit of the learner but also for the benefit of the organization for which the learner works.

1.2 HOW THE MENTOR HELPS THE LEARNER

We shall explore the mentor's role in the particular case of the *Trainer Development Programme* in later sections, but firstly we will look at the mentor's role in general. Module TDS 6, *Mentoring*, has been written specifically on this subject but here we will give a brief overview.

An effective mentor provides support in two main ways, by helping the learner to:

- gain the necessary qualifications;
- achieve progress in the workplace.

More specifically, they do this by helping the learner to:

- identify their current level of competence;
- plan an appropriate programme of study;
- collect suitable evidence of competence;
- advise on work-related activities and assignments, both from a general perspective and according to how they can provide evidence for an S/NVQ;
- gain access to areas within the organization that may otherwise be closed to them;
- identify key decision makers within the organization.

1.3 WHAT MAKES AN EFFECTIVE MENTOR?

To be effective, a mentor should be:

- well organized, accessible and committed to personal development;
- respected by the learner and others within the organization;
- able to maintain confidentiality at all times;
- experienced in giving support and counsel;
- interested in the development of people;
- able to communicate easily with both the learner and the line manager concerned;
- working in a similar or complementary area to the person they are mentoring;
- knowledgeable and positive about the organization, how it works and where it is going.

Sadly, not everyone has the natural attributes needed in a mentor, and if you feel that you lack any of these qualities it would be best if you suggested to the learner that they find someone else to mentor them. However, because of their interest in the career development needs of employees within the organization, HRD managers often make very effective mentors. Similarly, past learners, that is people who have worked through a similar kind of open learning programme, also often have naturally good mentoring skills (having been through the process themselves) and are therefore able to empathise with the learner.

On the other hand, effective mentoring also requires practice – even amongst those who have the necessary natural attributes. If you suspect that you lack the necessary practical expertise in mentoring, working through some or all of Module TDS 6, *Mentoring* will help you. In particular, the Workplace Activities in Part 2, The Process of Mentoring and Part 4, Managing the Process should give some experience of what is involved in mentoring.

1.4 HOW THE MENTORING RELATIONSHIP SHOULD WORK

It is important that the mentor is someone **not** directly involved with the learner's work, i.e. line manager or supervisor, as there is a possibility that the roles can become confused. It must be remembered at all times that the mentor is responsible for helping with the professional and personal development of the learner and that mentoring is outside the normal boss/subordinate relationship.

The mentor must clearly define the relationship at the outset, i.e. the mentor is there to 'help' not 'tell', and the learner's own manager should be kept informed of the learner's activities.

The learner must be assured that a code of confidentiality will be maintained, as not all problems will be related to study. There may be work-related or personal problems to overcome during the relationship.

Not all mentor/learner relationships are guaranteed to be successful, especially if either party does not have the flexibility to choose their 'partner'. This is not a failing on either side, and the best thing to do is to withdraw from the partnership and re-negotiate, without hard feelings on either side.

1.5 PLANNING THE MENTORING

Mentoring is not an activity which has set time-scales. The time invested by all parties is substantial, and may be for as along as the learner benefits from it.

It is good practice to schedule regular meetings, with the mentor taking the initiative to arrange a preliminary meeting to discuss the learner's expectations and agree objectives.

In the early stages it is beneficial to both parties to schedule regular progress review meetings, either weekly or fortnightly, and establish a time-table for project work, assignments, etc. About 1–2 hours per month is recognized as the average for meetings, but there may need to be more at the start. The time between meetings can be extended as the partnership progresses.

It takes time to build trust between two people and after about six months a meeting should be arranged to review the relationship. At this point both parties may agree to either strengthen, or terminate, the relationship, and may well draw up an agreed action plan covering future mentoring arrangements.

PART 2
What the Mentor Needs to Know

INTRODUCTION

You may well find that even before they start to work through the course materials, the learner you are mentoring has a number of questions about the *Trainer Development Programme* itself and what it will demand of them. If the learner is new to open learning, there may also be concerns about the processes involved in this approach. Some learners who are seeking specific qualifications will certainly want to know about S/NVQs, competence-based training, the correct procedures for providing evidence and so on.

This section therefore contains most of the essential information you need to help your learner resolve any problems they may have about the *Trainer Development Programme* and the open learning method of study, while Part 3 covers the S/NVQ system. We suggest that you read both Parts in conjunction with the *User Guide*.

2.1 HOW THE PROGRAMME IS STRUCTURED

The *Trainer Development Programme* consists of self-study, open learning style modules, comprising print-based materials and, in the case of part of the *Programme*, audio cassettes.

It is an open learning programme, which means that the teaching element is built into the material, although the learner will also have more personal support. The material is also work-oriented and contains many Workplace Activities which enable the development of workplace skills.

The complete *Trainer Development Programme* consists of three series:

Assessment of NVQs and SVQs series, 9 modules

For those responsible for assessing S/NVQ candidates and those monitoring the S/NVQ system.

Training Delivery series, 7 modules

For those involved in the delivery of training on a one to one or small group basis;

Training Design and Management series, 6 modules

For those involved in training in its broader context (i.e. planning and designing training for an organization).

A complete list of all modules, with a brief description of their contents is given in Section 2.3

2.2 THE POTENTIAL USES OF THE PROGRAMME

Each module in the *Trainer Development Programme* stands alone and does not have to be used in conjunction with any other module. They can be used in any order to suit the learner's individual needs.

The modules of the *Trainer Development Programme* can be used in a number of ways:

- as individual modules on one topic for self-development;

- to assist the development of skills and abilities to achieve new organizational goals;

- as the basis for a short course;

- as a combination of modules to meet the requirements of a qualification, as described in Part 6 of the *User Guide,* for example:

  - the traditional ITD Certificate in Training and Development;

  - the competence-based ITD Direct Trainers Award and Certificate in Human Resource Development;

  - the Training and Development Lead Body S/NVQ Level 3 and 4;

  - the full range of TDLB Assessor and Verifier Awards.

Addresses for all organizations offering these awards can be found in the *User Guide,* which also includes a matrix linking the modules to the first generation of S/NVQs. Later editions of the *User Guide* will link the modules to the new Standards in the same way. As a mentor one of your most important responsibilities will be to guide your learner through these qualifications, so make yourself familiar with them now.

2.3 A BRIEF SYNOPSIS OF EACH MODULE

The *Trainer Development Programme* comprises three series totalling 22 modules, the contents of which are outlined below.

Assessment of NVQs and SVQs series

Aimed at assessors and verifiers of NVQs and SVQs. Study time: approximately 7–10 hours per module.

Module 1, Introduction to the NVQ System

An overview of the NVQ system, why it has come into being, what it is, and what it seeks to achieve. Aimed at all involved in the NVQ system.

Module 2, Designing Assessment Systems

Help with understanding and applying the principles of competence-based assessment as well as deciding on the range of evidence required and how it might be collected. Aimed at assessors.

Module 3, Workplace Assessment

How to assess a candidate's competence against the standards specified for an NVQ award through observation of performance in the workplace. Aimed at the assessor in the workplace.

Module 4, Second Line Assessment and APL (Accreditation of Prior Learning)

How to assess the competence of a candidate using a more diverse range of evidence, including evidence of past workplace achievement. Aimed at the second line assessor.

Module 5, Internal Verification

How to monitor the assessment of candidates carried out by assessors within your organization, and hence ensure that the assessment process is consistent and reliable. Aimed at verifiers working within an organization.

Module 6, External Verification

How to use the external verification process to support the work of internal verifiers by ensuring that the quality of assessment of candidates meets awarding body standards. Aimed at verifiers working on behalf of an awarding body.

Module 7, APL Advisers

How to help and advise candidates seeking to obtain an NVQ using evidence of their past achievements in the workplace. Aimed at APL advisers.

Module 8, Quality Assurance and NVQ

Explains the principles of quality assurance which are central to the NVQ standards and the assessment of the NVQ process, and helps you to apply these principles in your organization. Aimed at assessors.

Module 9, Achieving your NVQ

Particularly for candidates for NVQs, this module explains the NVQ process, and helps identify which NVQ is relevant to them, and to decide what evidence they need to present to attain the award. Aimed at candidates.

Training Delivery series

For those involved in the delivery of training to individuals or small groups. Study time: approximately 10–12 hours per module, with additional work on Workplace Activities.

Module 1, Introduction to Training and Development

Discusses what training is and why it matters. It examines what is involved in adopting a systematic approach to training and explores the role of the manager and training specialist. It also looks at the influences on training from government, examining and awarding bodies, and education and training providers.

Module 2, Learning and the Role of the Trainer

Focuses on how the trainer can help people to learn. It examines the principles of learning and explains how the concept of the learning unit can be used to design and deliver effective training. It also analyses the role of the trainer and suggests how the trainer's role may be developed.

Module 3, Identifying Learning Needs

Focuses on the importance of identifying learning needs in the planning and design of training events. It explores a range of approaches and techniques for identifying the learning needs of both individuals and groups, and explains how these approaches and techniques can be related to organizational needs.

Module 4, Designing Individual and Group Learning

Provides guidance on designing and planning a learning strategy to meet the identified needs of individuals and small groups, as well as a detailed look at the various training methods from the point of view of the trainer planning and designing the learning event.

Module 5, Delivering Individual and Group Learning

Focuses on how effective training can be delivered. It describes the types of learning material and equipment available to the trainer and explores the most common methods of delivery. It also looks at group behaviour theories and examines the trainer's role in facilitating open and distance learning.

Module 6, Mentoring

Focuses on the role of the mentor in training and development programmes. It describes the process of mentoring, discusses the benefits of a mentoring system, and examines the skills required by a mentor and how they may be developed.

Module 7, Evaluating Learning Outcomes

Looks at how the effectiveness of training can be measured. It considers why we should assess effectiveness and examines specific evaluation techniques available to the trainer. It also explains the role of evaluation in modifying and adapting learning events, and discusses how to give and receive feedback.

Training Design and Management series

For those involved in training in the broader context of planning and designing training for an organization. Study time: approximately 10–12 hours per module, with additional work on Workplace Activities.

Module 1, Organizational Training and Development Needs

Explores the relationship between the organization and the training and development function. It looks particularly at how the culture and structure of an organization influences training and development, the contribution of training to business planning, the influence of organizational structure on trainer roles, and finally, key techniques for analysing organizational training and development needs.

Module 2, Operational Planning for Training

Explains how to produce operational plans for training and development to conform with agreed business strategies. It looks particularly at business planning, at the resource implications of business planning, and at methods, systems and budget implications of training plans, and at how to present those plans.

Module 4, Managing Training Resources and Learner Support

Gives guidance on how to obtain and effectively manage resources to carry out training and support the learning of individuals and groups. It also looks at the recruitment of trainees (such as apprentices and graduates), how to negotiate roles, evaluate and select training locations, hardware, software and systems, as well as at the issue of self managed learning.

Module 5, Evaluating Training and Development

Offers guidance and practice in planning, setting up and carrying out the evaluation of training and development programmes, in terms of meeting the learning needs of those concerned and of cost effectiveness to the organization. It also examines the techniques available to carry out evaluation, concentrating on the outcomes at the level of job performance and team/department/organizational effectiveness.

Module 6, Strategies for Change

Looks at the role of the trainer as a change agent and in managing change. It examines how and why change occurs and how to bring about change smoothly and successfully; finally, it looks at change within the training profession itself, concentrating particularly on trainer roles and also technological development.

2.4 THE OPEN LEARNING APPROACH

The basis of the *Trainer Development Programme* is the learning modules. They are thorough and detailed, and the open learning approach allows the learner the maximum of flexibility and the freedom to choose:

- how much to study;

- in what detail;

- when to study;

- how long to take.

The learners select the modules which best fit their development needs and study on their own, as open learning is basically 'tutorial in print'. The text is written in such a way that it frequently:

- asks the learner questions;

- encourages the learner to undertake activities rather than read passively;

- provides feedback to the learner's responses;

- enables the learner to check on their progress.

All the workbooks contain the following features:

- learning objectives at the beginning of the workbook and each section;

- Activities in the form of hypothetical questions or tasks requiring responses;

- Workplace Activities providing the learners with opportunities to practice their skills in the workplace;

- progress checks to enable learners to assess themselves against the objectives;

- Self Checks or mini-tests for assessing whether the main points of the text have been grasped before proceeding further.

The audio cassettes which accompany each module also contain Case Studies and Reflections, which give the learner the opportunity to reflect upon the topics covered and carry out a progress self-assessment.

Because the learning material takes the place of a tutor, the mentor can support the learner by:

- helping the learner identify learning needs;

- providing guidance on various learning opportunities available within the learner's development programme and organization;

- helping the learner to gain access to internal people and systems which can assist them in acquiring and applying learning in the workplace;

- giving advice on Workplace Activities.

This kind of practical help is particularly important for a learner using the *Trainer Development Programme* materials, as here the mentor needs to support the open learning process by for example:

- planning a route through the programme with the learner, using the descriptions of module contents and qualifications contained in the *User Guide*;

- arranging for the learner to attend workshops arranged by the local centre;

- arranging work placements for any learner who is not currently in work or lacks sufficient experience.

The *User Guide* contains a list of Approved Development and Assessment Centres (ADACs) which can provide support for learners wishing to gain an ITD award.

2.5 S/NVQ LEVELS AND ASSOCIATED QUALIFICATIONS

The *Trainer Development Programme* covers the following qualifications and S/NVQ levels:

Assessment of NVQs and SVQs series

Institute of Training and Development (ITD)

- External Verifier Award
- Internal Verifier Award
- Portfolio S/NVQ Assessor Award
- APL Assessor Award
- APL Adviser Award
- Workplace Coach/First Line Assessor Award

City and Guilds (C&G)

- Skills Assessor Award
- Vocational Assessor Award
- APL Adviser Award
- Internal Verifier Award
- External Verifier Award
- Skills Trainer and Assessor Award
- Vocational Trainer and Assessor Award

Pitmans Examination Institute (PEI)

- Assessor Award with Verification Units

Royal Society of Arts (RSA)

- Assessor Award

- APL Adviser Award

- Internal Verifier Award

Business and Technology Education Council (BTEC)

- Modules for Assessment and Verification

London Chamber of Commerce and Industry (LCCI)

- Modules for Assessment and Verification

Training Delivery series

- Syllabus-based ITD Certificate in Training and Development;

- First generation S/NVQ in Training and Development at Level 3;

- Competence-based ITD Direct Trainers Award (N/SVQ Level 3 plus two additional ITD units);

- Proposed second generation S/NVQ in Learning Support (Level 3) and Learner Support and Management (Level 4) and Human Resource Development (Level 4);

- ITD Professional Development Programme (available from January 1995).

Training Design and Management series

- Syllabus-based ITD Certificate in Training and Development;

- First generation S/NVQ in Training and Development at Level 4;

- Competence-based ITD Certificate in Human Resource Development (S/NVQ Level 4 plus four additional ITD units and three MCI M1 units);

- S/NVQ in Training and Development at Level 4 – Design and Delivery;

- Proposed second generation S/NVQ in Learning Support (Level 3) and in Learner Support and Management (Level 4) and Human Resource Development (Level 4);

- ITD Professional Development Programme (available from January 1995).

The S/NVQs are offered by ITD, C&G, BTEC, RSA, PEI and SCOTVEC.

This information is correct at the time of going to press. However, to establish the exact position with regard to the S/NVQs and the *Trainer Development Programme*, please contact your local centre as the standards may change.

PART 3
The S/NVQ System

INTRODUCTION

The purpose of this Part is to explain the principles behind the S/NVQ system, and the process whereby an S/NVQ is awarded. Some learners using this *Programme* may wish to use it as part of a programme which relates to TDLB standards, either for an S/NVQ or as part of a standards-related trainer training programme.

3.1 WHAT ARE S/NVQs?

S/NVQs are qualifications that relate to work, based on standards of competence set by industry. They are concerned with outcomes, or results, not the process of learning, and are awarded as a result of competence-based assessment in the workplace. Unlike other qualifications there are no formal entry requirements and previous experience is taken into consideration. Also there are no time constraints.

S/NVQs are awarded by established awarding bodies such as City and Guilds of London Institute and professional bodies such as the Institute of Training and Development, following standards established by industry lead bodies.

An S/NVQ in Training and Development is a nationally recognised qualification, which is based on standards of knowledge and practical ability set by the TDLB (Training and Development Lead Body), the lead body for the training industry.

3.2 THE PRINCIPLES BEHIND S/NVQs AND WORK-BASED COMPETENCE

Each S/NVQ comprises a number of units of competence which set out the standards that must be achieved, and demonstrated, in the workplace. Within each unit are a linked series of components, or elements of competence. Each unit is a mini qualification in its own right and the learner can receive credit for each unit completed, following an assessment of competence in carrying out the occupational competence in the workplace. However an S/NVQ can only be awarded if all the standards are satisfied.

3.3 THE BENEFITS TO INDIVIDUALS AND ORGANIZATIONS

S/NVQs give the learner the opportunity to work towards a nationally recognised qualification at their own pace. They give recognition for tasks undertaken within the workplace, and there are no set examinations or time limits on the collection of evidence or attainment of the award.

The benefits to organizations of S/NVQs are that they provide a better trained, more confident and productive workforce. S/NVQs provide a means of measuring how the performance of staff meets the organization's requirements, without taking staff away from their normal work activities. As S/NVQs are employment-related they are independent of any particular training or learning programmes, and because the standards are defined by statements of competence, they are totally relevant to the workplace.

3.4 THE PROCESS OF COMPILING A PORTFOLIO

Learners working towards an S/NVQ will need to generate a portfolio of evidence, that is a personal collection of evidence of their performance at work, which they will need to present to the Assessor as part of the final assessment for the S/NVQ concerned.

Portfolios also enable learners to manage their own learning and personal development more efficiently. They are a means whereby the learners record their experiences and achievements.

To create a portfolio the learner first has to look at their own strengths and weaknesses by comparing their own personal profile against the demands of the job. This will help them identify their own development and learning plan based on priorities and needs, reflecting not only what is necessary but what is possible and achievable. An Action Plan is then drawn up to demonstrate how the learner will provide evidence of new competence. The contents of the Action Plan then dictate the route by which the portfolio of acceptable evidence of competence is compiled. The mentor's role here will be to discuss the learner's self-assessment of competence, and if necessary, advise on the priority areas which need to be developed.

The *User Guide,* and *Assessment of NVQs and SVQs* series Module 9, *Achieving your NVQ,* explain in more detail exactly what is involved in compiling a portfolio and how it relates to the various systems of accreditation.

3.5 THE CRITERIA FOR ACCEPTABLE EVIDENCE

The portfolio must provide evidence of competence in all the relevant units and elements being claimed, and it must be of appropriate quality.

Evidence should be as recent as possible, but in any event should always bear the date of origin.

It should be authentic as it must prove that it has been produced by the learner and therefore, will need to be endorsed by the learner's manager or colleagues, for example.

The exact requirements needed to meet the various specifications for acceptable evidence are discussed more fully in the *User Guide,* and in Modules 3 and 4 of the *Assessment of NVQs and SVQs* series.

3.6 THE ASSESSMENT PROCESS

When the evidence is neatly filed and labelled the portfolio is presented to an Assessor. If the Assessor considers the evidence sufficient a formal interview is arranged to confirm that the evidence is sufficient and valid. If the interview proves satisfactory the Assessor will confirm the award.

If, for some reason, the Assessor does not consider the evidence sufficient, the learner will be advised to undertake extra work before re-presenting the portfolio.

PART 4
How the Mentor can Provide Support

INTRODUCTION

The career and personal development of a learner is strongly influenced by the relationship with the mentor. The support of the mentor, therefore, is often very important for assisting and stimulating the learner's development.

Just as there are many ways of supporting the learner, so there are a variety of methods by which learners can develop, and these will vary according to the objectives of the training programme concerned. The purpose of this section is therefore to suggest particular ways in which a mentor can help a learner on the *Trainer Development Programme*.

4.1 OPEN LEARNING

Some people get a feeling of isolation when studying using the open learning method. The mentor can provide support by maintaining regular contact with the learner. This allows the mentor to establish whether or not the learner is managing to keep up with the study schedule they agreed prior to commencing the course.

The mentor must also be able to reassure learners if they get anxious regarding some area of their course. For example, they may need to seek support and help from the mentor because they are apprehensive about undertaking a Workplace Activity. More particularly, in open learning the mentor should be an easily accessible source of feedback to an otherwise isolated learner who probably has a regular need to discuss various matters relating to both specific material within the workbooks and the programme as a whole – sometimes at quite short notice. An unsupported learner also often encounters considerable difficulties in finding places on workshops and work placement schemes. In this situation, a respected independent mentor who knows their way around the organization can give invaluable help to the learner by acting as a source of information on suitable workshop events and openings for work experience and by putting the learner in contact with other useful sources of knowledge.

4.2 S/NVQs

The first task for anyone who wishes to aim for an S/NVQ is to assess those areas in which further development is needed and those where present or previous experience will help in providing evidence. The mentor can help in this process.

By using the information in the *User Guide*, the mentor and learner can together plan how to go about gathering evidence against specific elements of competence, and plan a programme of study. The mentor may also be able to provide advice on how the learner should tackle a work-related task in order to provide suitable evidence of competence and also recommend relevant sources of information at the workplace.

The ways in which the mentor can assist a candidate for an S/NVQ can be summarised as follows:

- helping to guide the learner through the necessary competences;
- helping the learner to collect acceptable evidence and bring it together in a portfolio that reflects the learner's competence accurately;
- supporting the learner during the assessment process;
- motivating the learner to complete the programme.

4.3 PLANNING TRAINING PROGRAMMES

The mentor can support both general and qualification training programmes by helping the learner identify their overall aims and how the *Trainer Development Programme* can help fulfil these aims. In this way, the mentor takes on the role of a training needs assessor, and the mentor's knowledge of the overall contents of the *Programme* can be used to guide the learner towards the most suitable training plan. The different ways in which the *Programme* can be used to meet specific training requirements are detailed in Parts 3 and 4 of the *User Guide*, so refer to this information as necessary. It outlines the different demands made on the learner by both traditional and standards-based training and by trainer training linked to specific business needs, all of which need to be taken into consideration when the mentor becomes involved in training needs analysis and planning individual training programmes.